Sweet Cultivation

Sweet Cultivation

Allia Dahmes

ISBN: 1092194150
ISBN-13: 978-1092194150

A collection of poetry and prose about God and surviving the beautiful chaos called life.

From the heart of a temporary traveler to another,
may the words create constellations
like never before.

Bismillah ar-Rahman ar-Rahim

In the name of Allah, the most Gracious, the most Merciful.

All praise is due to most High,

Without Him, I am nothing.

Without His mercy and guidance, none of this would be possible.

I hoped for a stem to stick out and
in beautiful endurance
my first petals appeared.
So as I watered my inner self over and over,
the nourishing smell of individuality arose.
A secluded yet determined soul had risen from
temptation
from the depths of my roots
I finally became vulnerable,
a temptation to live peacefully and freely
in a field of the ungrown.

My fear is not
people who choose to leave,
it is the choice
of leaving myself.
The fear lies not
in temporary and promised loss,
it lies in the focal point of survival.

الغرباء

I am walking a journey of what people think are strange
things.
I am a stranger
even amongst my own.
But as the beloved (peace be upon him) said,
blessed are the strangers.

Al Gurabaa: The strangers

I am trying to become not only who I want to be,
but a devoted slave to the Most High Who will be pleased
with me.
No self destruction
just my soul and His decree.
I once took the road less traveled,
migrated tear drops
that could make up a smooth sailing sea.
The dunya was not a punishment from a tree,
for the first to walk on earth,
peace be upon he.
For purpose of this place is not punishment,
it is finding true sanctuary in the Giver of life.
And so I made a plea
not a request
but a humble,
silent cry of
"Help me
don't deny me your paradise
ya Allah,
guide me to who You want me to be."

Embedded with genes of selflessness and sabr
from a home of sacrifice
to a land of gratitude

Sabr: patience

Self rituals:
Connect with your heart.
Bathe in beautiful patience.
Let prostration be your exercise.

You were not created of 206 bones,
to carry a weight of the world as a burden.

And when the waves hit,
don't let that stop you from sailing.
Perhaps they could test you
to explore shores beyond count
in a midst of beautiful chaos.

The devaluation of women has become a disease,
contagious amongst society,
a cancer in culture.
They don't find the cure
because they choose not to.
For years
and years
and still they fight.
Yet, her rights were given over 1400 years ago.
Women have been honored.
Women are honored.
Heaven lies under a mother's feet.
A woman
is a school
once you teach her,
she can teach generations.
A woman
is a warrior,
only she can feel
two hearts beat as one.
A woman
is the sun that compliments the moon.
Without him, there is no her.
Without her, there is no him.
So tell me,
what has really valued women
from the beginning of submission
in which was spread
by the best of mankind?
Implement.
Tell them.
Tell them all.

The art of letting go
is accepting what was
by comparing who you were
to the present self.
Make the lessons count.
Every single one of them.

Stop building homes in people. Stop depending on temporary souls to fill your heart. When you depend on a person to make you feel whole and they leave, what is left? Emptiness. You'll have to pick yourself back up and connect the broken pieces together. We need a foundation that keeps us grounded.
A foundation that will never break us.
For the One that mends
will never disappoint.

قلب

Made to love unconditionally
like a cushion it was created,
soft,
pure,
ever so delicate.
To when one hand touches it,
it has a power so contagious.
Love as if there is no other option,
as if it is all you know.
Love yourself enough that
toleration is not inferiority.
Protect it.
Take good care of the gift.
Don't let them throw it away.

Qalb: Heart

These burdens you carry
could be your silent killers
waiting to see you burn,
flame after flame.
This clear vision
you were meant to find
is but from a near distance.
So close
you could seize it.
So far
you could mourn it.
You can see it,
can you?
A short glimpse
and your mind will be at rest.
That minuscule gleam you constantly watch
through the rear view mirrors of your soul
is more than just enough.
These burdens you carry
could be your weapons of hope.
Breathe . . .
for the light awaits you.

Loneliness is not misery, it is contentment. It is embracing the richness of solitude. It is loving your own company. It is connecting with your thoughts and emotions. It is purifying the mind and heart. No one else but you can attain self knowledge and its beauty.

The words I tell others are love letters to myself.
The walls I've built aren't walls anymore
they've reached its highest peak
transformed into skyscrapers.
So I complain my sorrows and grief
to my Creator,
and I continue to write love letters
to the person who knows me best.

فقر

It sucks me in its deceiving enjoyment,
my desires become a sickness.
Every time I find the cure,
it tries to come back again.
I am poor to worldly possessions.
They don't want me to win,
and sometimes I let it take the lead.
This burden I carry on my shoulders
has reached the inner cores of my stomach.
A hunger strike has approached
I am poor
to my Lord.
The starvation comes from a soul
whose emptiness is only filled
when His remembrance becomes its breakfast
patience become its lunch
and gratitude becomes its dinner.

Fiqr: Poverty

Never forget,
you are a poem
that breathes metaphors.
With a soul shaped by stories
in which one day people will enter
and highlight the good bits
but never leave the bad ones,
to accept and love them too.
With a heart formed in pages
never to be ripped and thrown,
instead welcomed with bookmarks
that leave others overwhelmed
by the love it brings.
You are an art piece
my dear,
meant to embraced
in everything that you are.

أمي

She's clothed in beautiful patience,
she makes it look so easy for the world to see.
At the back of my mind I say,
"Mama, how do you do it?"
I wish I could utter those words to her,
but words will turn into rivers.
What I know is,
her Lord knows it all.
With every silent cry
she holds on to His rope
and by His will and mercy
He never lets go.
Every
single
time.

Ummi: My mother

O soul,
wait a little longer
grip a little tighter.

My Lord,
I am sorry for the sins that You only see.
You gifted me sight,
hearing,
and a mind to believe
In You I seek refuge
and belief in your decree.
You show me signs to keep sailing
in this world of misery
You saved me time and time again,
how blind could I be
to not realize Your mercy is bigger
than every ocean and splendid sea?
I come to You helpless
You come to me unempty
for the love You have for Your slave is incomparable,
infinite,
ever so richly.

الرحيم

If I could only count how many times
I asked for just a rain drop to touch my roots
and instead I grew petals
by the showers of His mercy.

Ar Raheem: the most Merciful 2/99

Pain is inevitable but so is breaking through it. Visit the places you never imagined yourself visiting. It's going to be uncomfortable, but you must invite pain and not let it invite you.

There is no timeline in healing. Let your heart take its sweet time. Explore the world within. Shower your wounds with care. Everyone's healing process is different. Keep unfolding the layers, there is no destination. It is just another journey within a journey.

توكل

We plan and do more planning,
as if the pages are blank
and His planning is not enough.
The pen has already been lifted
the pages are currently turning.
It is His plan we must trust.

Tawwakul: Trust in [the Al Mighty]

Delve into authenticity
shine in self acceptance
let them both be the beautiful promises you can't break.

You are created in the best of forms.
Do not let society undervalue you.
You are more than your appearance.
You are the creation of the One that creates beauty.
Let that be enough.
You are
enough.

On my downfalls,
You pick me up.
In weakness,
You give me strength.
You clothe me in patience and reassure me of Your
mercy
by the remembrance of Your noble words.
And Your love; oh Your love..
infinite
enumerated.
rich.
so grand.
Your friendship,
there's no Beloved Friend like You in the world.
When I talk to You,
sometimes I don't have to say a word,
and other times the tears in prostration are a language
in itself,
a power of your closeness.
When the weight of this temporary world sets on my
shoulders, You remind me that the fight is continuous.
That this tug of war hasn't ended just yet
to pull harder
and hold on to Your rope.
That there's ease within
and after every hardship.
That You know my potential of survival in this crazy
sphere
and I'm slowly finding it
day by day.

Part of healing
is accepting that healing is layers.
Commit to the unfolding
for you are made entirely stitched of utter greatness.
Your growth is to be embraced
in light,
not concealed
in darkness.

My heart has traveled places
and in counting
it still wanders.
This heart of mine has swam oceans,
yet wave after wave
His mercy saved me.
This heart of mine has climbed and stumbled,
yet in quitting
His love embraced me.
This heart of mine has reached other hearts,
yet in disappointment
His light never left me.
And in counting
it still wanders.

I am among roses with mended petals.
Roots playing tug of war in concrete.
With a stem holding on for dear life.
Sometimes surrounded by a rainstorm that interrupts
yet intensifies my growth,
and sometimes surrounded by sunshine that helps me
stand firm.

War Torn Child

The land is tired,
even the oceans run away.
The dry sands can't even feed themselves,
from the blood that stains its every grain.
The blood of a mother who was sniped, leaving her
child in tears and pain.
Questioning the enemies of humanity,
but her father can't explain.
"My sweetheart," he says,
"with Allah her soul remains.
The tyrants will soon be trapped in chains of the fire,
with guilt running through their veins."
She says,
"I just want to sleep in peace, just one time, my heart
can not contain,
my lullabies are loud bombs being dropped,
plane after plane.
What is it that they gain,
from giving us so much pain?
Our neighbors need aid and a comfy home to stay,
our neighbors can't escape the shootings
and missiles that come their way.
Our neighbors of other borders are starving day by day.
Does the world know
or are they silent?
What peace do they portray?
Where is my childhood?
I just want to laugh and play,
my friends and I cry and hug,
as we wait for a good day.
But the world has failed us,
how much does the burden weigh?"

Her father replied once more,
"We bear a little longer,
for our Lord will know the way,
and if a home here isn't granted,
in jannah you will play.
Allah will reunite you with mama,
and the pain will go away.
And to those who caused this long nightmare,
they will see on Judgement Day.
Just hold on my love,
Allah hears the duas that we say.
We will be free one day,
even though the world isn't our permanent stay.
For every drop
of blood and tear
they will pay for the ruins of today.
Because the land is tired too,
even the oceans run away."

When we fully realize that this life comes in cycles, we will have less expectations and disappointments.
We'll continue to be showered with hardships, gifted with blessings, and rewarded with lessons.
What we learn from them is what molds us into who we are and what we could potentially become.

The only fragility to conform in
is to break in pieces
for peace.

Time Heals

They say that time heals all wounds.
But has your soul yet been in tune?
These storms just keep on coming and I really have no
clue.
I'm not ready for this change,
the evil whispers scream too soon.
But my mind and heart have traveled a distance so far
apart,
there's no place for me to bloom.
I try,
I truly do.
This heart of mine doesn't lie
but these battles that I fight
these internal silent cries.
And the pain that I've neglected from feeling for so
long have turned these
dark brown eyes
into fragile glassed windows aiming to ignite
every fall and every fight,
yet in every stumble I still rise.
All due to the *most Merciful*,
the *most Loving,*
the *most High.*
I promise you,
time heals for His timing is only to imply
that His mercy is far greater every single time.
So dear soul,
don't you cry,
your faith shall never die.

You are not your pain, you are not your battles, you are
not these times that you despise.
You are merely a wanderer and as you travel you will
trip
over
and over again.
And with time
you will only rise.

Hardships will knock on your door, people will come into your life unexpectedly, all with the purpose of teaching us something. Do not neglect the wisdom life could bring. For these gifts are part of surviving this chaos.

You have taught me to grow wise beyond my years. From practicing beautiful patience, to implementing the importance of doing things with good intentions.
Your sacrifice is never forgotten.
Your arms keep me warm in a cold world.
You are put in a status to where my gateway to paradise would be the reason of my treatment to you.
You fulfill the large pieces of my heart.
My sadness is yours, your happiness is mine.
I can't imagine a world without you, but it is He we belong to and to Him we all return.
I hope that I make you proud.
You don't deserve this temporary world,
you deserve the highest rank of paradise and everything in it.
My supplications to the Creator of you and I are a language of my unconditional love towards you.
May mercy forever be upon you.

"And your Lord has decreed that you not worship except Him, and to parents, good treatment. Whether one or both of them reach old age [while] with you, say not to them [so much as], "uff," and do not repel them but speak to them a noble word." [17:23]

"And lower to them the wing of humility out of mercy and say, "My Lord, have mercy upon them as they brought me up [when I was] small." [17:24]

To the world you are another option
but to your Lord you are valuable
of His forgiveness
Mercy
and infinite love.
Do not doubt the Master of the heavens and the earth.
For He never neglects
nor forgets.

I would often wonder why forgiveness is a challenge. To then realize that we make it difficult depending on our reaction. Forgiving is not excusing one's actions, nor does it mean what a person did was okay. To forgive, is to grow. To forgive, is allowing yourself to mend your heart and not harden it. It is for you and no one else.

How ungrateful is it to ask, "Why me?"
When You chose me
to be a survivor
of endless circumstances.
You showered me with storms
knowing the sun will always shine.
And by Your mercy,
my roots have made fruits of wisdom.
So I tell myself,
how could I forget
that I was promised ease
by the One that makes it so easy?

Empathy is one of the most powerful assets we could possess. The simple ability of understanding the feelings and thoughts of another is a sign of coexistence, love, and compassion. Empathy makes the world go round.
Let gentleness be your noise.

Words aimed as bullets to the heart of another,
no hesitation of what one could truly suffer.
The hands carry dirt of internal clutter,
a toxic mind
a cold heart of no recover.
You call it love
yet how dare you seem to utter,
false hope when you come at her
like thunder?
A hazy spirit
ready for demons to uncover,
towards an elder man's precious,
helpless daughter.
There's a Lord
that is the ultimate Preserver,
loving those that treat His creation gently
to attain His pleasure.
His mercy is of no comparable measure.
For He dislikes the nature of an abuser,
an unfearful,
cold oppressor.

One day,
the light will prevail.
The universe within will make sense.
The constellations will appear.
It'll all be clear in due time.

In a world of half heartedness,
be the love you want to receive.
Love in full,
even when they decide to love you in halves.

Without religion,
I'd be of no purpose.
I wouldn't know that giving a smile
is an act of charity.
Nor will I learn that
determination plays a role,
to fill up one side of the scale
by constructing a better home
that isn't this world.

I quickly swam oceans to catch up
wave after wave,
not realizing
it is He that makes the waves move in motion.
For not even a leaf falls
without His knowledge.

Allia Dahmes

هجرة

I buried old parts of me,
walked past stained foot prints,
to travel lands of the unknown.
That later became my territories.

Hijrah: Migration

We sin and He forgives,
neglect yet He remembers,
lend our hand in times of hopelessness
yet returns in an arm's length
with immeasurable mercy and care.
There is no love truer than this,
there is none worthy of praise than Him.

There is no presence in human form,
that can ever compare to His closeness.
Closer to your jugular vein He says,
with a love that can build mountains.
A cure that heals the broken.
How close can one be to realize,
you're not alone
you never were,
you never will be.

The worldly life is a test on its own. The grades are our scales. You were put in this world because you can handle it. You will never be placed in a trial you can not survive from. For as long as you live on this ground, you can survive. From the storms that will try to pause your growth, to the winds that will try to stop you from walking. Look at how far you've come.

Keep going.
I know you're tired
but I promise,
the reward awaits
the blessings enumerate
His mercy remains.

النور

He tests you,
to mold you.
Blesses you,
to guide you.
Rewards you,
to please you.
Give praise to the One
that has promised ease.
Give thankfulness to the One
that wants to see you win.
For He is the Light.
And without light,
we tarnish.

An Noor: The Light | 93/99

There are those who choose to love half heartedly, then there are those who choose to love in full. When you love yourself enough to not tolerate half heartedness, you will learn to become whole.
You are no longer one tree, you become the whole garden.

Allia Dahmes

حلاوة الإيمان

These needy palms place the seeds,
as I let Him do the showering.
After every drop of His mercy
the roots loosened
and the ripeness was embraced.
What is more beloved
than to endeavor
ultimate sweetness?

Halawet al eeman: Sweetness of Faith

Let not one dare to underestimate the power
of your voice.
For it could make
an army.
A village.
An entire nation.

جنة

There is a home
better than this world
where rivers flow in harmony
and trails are traced by smiles
upon smiles.
Whatever you desire
is the reward
of fighting this temporary place.
There is a home
with satisfaction
beyond measures,
a point of no return
an enjoyment
for eternity.

Jannah: Paradise

We rise by lifting
not weakening.
We love by mending
not breaking.

Thanking the rewarder of Thankfulness
is a gift in itself.

قمر

I once asked the moon,
"Why is it when you come,
that sadness
and loneliness arrives?"
The moon responded,
"My dear,
you have the wrong idea.
For I rise
from darkness,
and one shall rise
from yours."

Qamar: Moon

Allia Dahmes

It's not clear to me that I have to be
a master of positivity
for we are imperfect beings
trying to find a way to believe
in ourselves
our ways
but firstly in the Al Mighty.
It's one thing to be free
but being imprisoned
in hardships is like
being caged in what seems permanent
when it is only temporary.
From sleeping on a cradle
to being placed in a cemetery.
I am only free
when I see
He is finally pleased with me.

Never doubt your potential of changing the world,
knowing your capabilities is already making the first step.
You are made of so much spark, you deserve to believe in
yourself when the world tries to stop you from doing it.
Prove them wrong and shine away.

The light touches darkness
yet in continues to rise.
And so will you
darling,
so will you.

Pain has been neglected time and time again.
This numbness stems from
the act of forgetting.
Stuck in a state of shock,
victimhood,
and misfortune.
The heart and mind have traveled miles apart.
They don't want anything to do with each other.
Nothing can pull them back together.
Until trauma stops pealing this sanity away.
These triggers consume me over and over.
And I let them win.
I respond with sorrow
and not peace.
Questioning,
When will the time come when grace grabs me by my
hand and says,
"It is your turn,
The sun has risen from this constant despair"
when will I stop living in this mind
and finally express
in wonderfully
tangible cycles?

Sometimes it's best to take a moment to yourself and think of where you are, where you're going, and where you want to be.

The chest feels heavy
a burden awaits to be lifted.
The bricks of what ifs and wishes
craves to be crumbled in pieces for peace.
The regrets and wanting for rewinds
will soon turn into gratitude
that will often remind.

Turn pain into power.
A thank you letter to keep for yourself could go a long way.

To the old friend,
thank you.
You taught me that my worth is placed
on the hands of not one soul.
For the first time
I found myself by putting me first.
I pray that you're always happy
even when I was blind to finding my own happiness
by putting yours before mine.
Thank you for the mishaps of opening up,
for teaching me
people should be worthy of my own vulnerability
and that I pick and choose.
When I now search for words of comfort,
I found my Lord to complain to on the way.

We feel empty even with the desires of this world. The luxuries are handed to us, the right people surrounds us and yet, there is still an emptiness that no one and nothing on this ground can fulfill.

The emptiness is a starving soul that has a longing for eternity. We are merely temporary travelers in a temporary place. We must fight for an everlasting that was promised to those who trade the pleasures of this world for the afterlife.

Dear little one,

I promise to let my arms
be your safe haven of comfort and tears.
To never emotionally and physically neglect you.
Never misunderstand you.
Always ask how your day was.
Remind you of your purpose.
Help you find synonyms of self love.
And to never,
ever abandon
your beautiful mind
and infinite potential.

Write the sorrows and happiness away,
but don't let the pen lift without gratitude.

O soul,
how many times will you let temporary pain consume
you?
You let it peel
your patience away
layer by layer.

I am capable. I matter. My voice is strength. I will not silence myself, nor will I let anyone silence me. My love is power. I deserve to love myself. I deserve to be loved the right way. I will make my dreams come true. My worth is not to be determined by society. I am not my downfalls.

Dear self,
please know.

They praise the bodies of insta-models and magazines
take a glimpse of a woman's body part because
"It was in front of me"
when they should know
lowering one's gaze is an act of worship
and her body is owned by the Creator of beauty.
You see,
there are those who support the ones that choose to dress
half naked
because "She is comfortable with her femininity".
But why is it that when I choose
to cover from my head to my toes
it's like a sin
to society?

جهاد

There is no struggle worse than fighting a battle within,
but what if I told you
that these battles are shaped in purpose
and not eternal suffering?
That they are not signs of weakness,
but to cultivate our strengths?

Jihad: Struggle [against one's self]

Self love is about loving the good, the bad, and the ugly. It is transforming your battle scars and turning them into beauty marks. It is accepting your flaws because, who doesn't have any? It is knowing your worth by walking away from things that don't serve you any good.

Every hardship you are granted, you can handle it. For He does not burden a soul beyond that it can bear. (2:286) and He promised ease not once, but twice. (94:5-6) You are meant to overcome the circumstances that are thrown at you. He knows we are capable, we just have to find it within ourselves. Despair not, for temporariness is the noise of this worldly life and the promise of the most Merciful is true.

We are so blinded by pain,
that we tend to block light from entering.
Just give one knock,
and His door will widely open.

It is You Who deserves my time
love
and energy.
Not a single soul will compare to the Friend You are to
me.
My Protector,
protect me and the ummah from the evil that we see.
Grant ease to the suffering who want to be free.
Guide us from this amusement
that does nothing but deceive,
and a soul that will always bounce back and retrieve.

May we be amongst those who strive for the permanent home and not grieve over the temporary.

You,
the one that hates looking in the mirror
the answer is within
can it get any clearer?
Your appearance is not meant to fit the standards of
society
don't let them shape you into what they want you to
be.
Be filled with confidence and self love,
something they don't want you to see.
And know that your worth is known by the Most
High,
the Creator of beauty.

We come across people who have once hurt us and have crossed our path with lessons, but it should not stop us from losing hope in others. It is our optimism that is dead, not humanity. How could we paint a majority based on our experiences with one person? If we continue to do that, we will not learn to think good of our future. So pray for good people to enter your life and pray that you grow into the person you want to meet.

I am not superhuman,
but love is powerful.
My love
is my power
and no one can take that away from me.

They say my Muslim identity is a threat
and so I tell them
indeed,
kindness and mercy could be threatening
in a world that doesn't seek it.

May this temporary abode
never stop you from seeking to find
the nutrients to bloom again.
A mission within
that transforms into experiences
that'll often remind.
An enjoyment
in which simplicity is the tune to the songs of your
heart.
Let not this journey be walked on
by somebody else.
These footprints are yours,
happiness awaits you.

Success lies in determination and believing in yourself. Once "I can't" turns to "I can" and "I can" turns to "I will" is implemented, you will become resilient. You become unbreakable.

Your love may be overwhelming, your kindness may be rare to come across, but that's the whole point. Rareness is not lost. It is treasured.

صديق

My beloved companion,
the pen has been lifted
by the Greatest of Writers.
Our pages have touched
by the grace of crossing.
When you enter the gardens by His will,
ask of me
as I will pray that I enter the greatest of places with
you.
For in paradise,
our hearts will rest
endurance will vanish.
Our shoulders will turn from
collecting each other's tears
to embracing weights being dropped
as we'll soak in
an atmosphere of
peace upon peace

God willing
God willing

Sadeeq: Friend

In the name of Allah
the One that ever so blessed me,
to be chosen of being your child
in the name of family.
You kissed my little bare feet
and used your arms to be homely,
your sacrifice is often remembered
as you were once lost and now caged free.
My gateway to paradise
how could I demean such status and authority,
to treat you well and love you so
as my Lord reminds in His book of
nobility?
Me without you is unimaginable
it is a world that I don't want to see,
but it is He we belong and return to
for we are merely travelers walking temporarily.
You do not deserve this world,
never
not this aching place of misery.
You deserve the highest rank of paradise,
a final abode for eternity.

Flee to the One that does the lifting,
your wings will land on purposeful places
your freedom is found through His grace.

Fir: Flee

Reflecting is the exercise of the mind
but actions are a commitment to flourish.

Self-pity is the root
of all failure.
Self-victimization is the epitome
of misery.
To dig deep
is evolution.
To acknowledge
is daring.

We are all walking metaphors
trying to find a way to construct a poem
that is our journey.

May you never feel the need to seek people's validation,
may the validation of yourself be the one that only matters.

I do not come from struggle,
I do not come from pain.
I was born pure
placed in a world of constant loss and gain.
I am not a victim of my affairs
or the circumstances that came my way,
I am a survivor of them all
because it is to my Lord that I pray.
It is Him that I belong to,
it is Him that I obey.
I am a traveler whose heart belongs to no place,
for I was once dust turned into the form of clay.

"Why do you write?"

I write because
it is easier to let the pen bleed
than my heart.
Because speaking isn't enough
and a blank canvas is the one that listens.

Garden your soul,
sprout graciously.
Not all flowers believe that they can stand for too long.

You are not lost, you are searching. Searching for a land of solace, a freedom of heart, a path to walk on. You are not the road bumps that aim to distract you, you are the direction that keeps you going.

We meet at a crossroads
share our ambitions
say a little prayer to one another.
We part ways,
come back to each other
the same repeats itself.
There is beauty when souls connect
in what we think is a big world.
This place is smaller than we think,
our hearts are close even from a distance.
And until then,
our roots will prepare to intertwine again.

Allia Dahmes

What has arrived is better for you than what is no longer present. There is beauty in parting ways with what no longer serves you any good. There is wisdom in knowing that in every goodbye, departure is one of the recipes to starting a new journey.

Forgive yourself. More than anything, remember that regret and self forgiveness is a sign of faith. A step to growth.

My Guide,
I have neglected You
over and over.
Forgetting how to please You
By the distractions of this worldly life.
My ultimate Forgiver,
Your forgiveness is what keeps the soul elevated.
May I never turn away from the grace of Your power.
May Your remembrance be the source of my mind and
heart.
For Your light encompasses all that exists.

The sky may be a limit,
but you are limitless.

They say the bigger the flower,
the less it consumes.
I say the richer the roots,
then the sweeter it blooms.
I give a thank you to the storms that enriched me,
you fooled me thinking it was a sign of constant misery.
These blessed petals grow in gratitude and humility,
may the harvest spread in wellness and prosperity.

Made in the USA
Middletown, DE
31 March 2023

27940152R00066